Working Together

Program Authors

Connie Juel, Ph.D.

Jeanne R. Paratore, Ed.D.

Deborah Simmons, Ph.D.

Sharon Vaughn, Ph.D.

PEARSON
Scott
Foresman

Glenview, Illinois
Boston, Massachusetts
Chandler, Arizona
Upper Saddle River, New Jersey

ISBN-13: 978-0-328-45275-0
ISBN-10:   0-328-45275-0

9 10 V011 14 13
CC1

Working Together

Contents

DANGER!

See page 25 for My New Words!

Let's Find Out

DANGER!

Chad and Mitch hunt for a spot to swim. Can they swim in this pond?

Stop! Much danger is in this pond. It is not a good pond to swim in. Chad and Mitch must hunt around for a spot to swim.

Whit hunts for a snack. She must check for danger. Can Whit munch this? Can Whit munch that? Stop! Nothing is fit to munch.

Whit must ask Mom. Mom has enough snacks that Whit can munch. Mom will fetch a snack that Whit can munch. Whit will munch and munch. Yum, yum!

Look at all eight. When must you check them? They tell that there is danger. Which tells not to set fire at camp?

When you swim, stop and think. Check it!
Is it a fit spot to swim?
When you munch, stop and think. Check it!
Is it fit to munch?

Danger on the Job

by Tori Casey

Which jobs have danger? Ben has danger on his job. Bugs are buzzing around. Buzzing bugs can sting. Check what Ben has on. Is it helping enough?

Jen is fixing a big crack. Jen has a drill.
Is drilling a danger? Check what Jen has on. Is
it helping?

Gus is standing up on top. Gus is not resting. Gus has a big branch to cut. Then he must cut eight others. Check what Gus has on. What is helping him?

Lots of kids are crossing. Tiff is helping them. Nothing will hit them. What is helping us see them?

FIRE
on the Hill

by Linda Miller   illustrated by Adam Gustavson

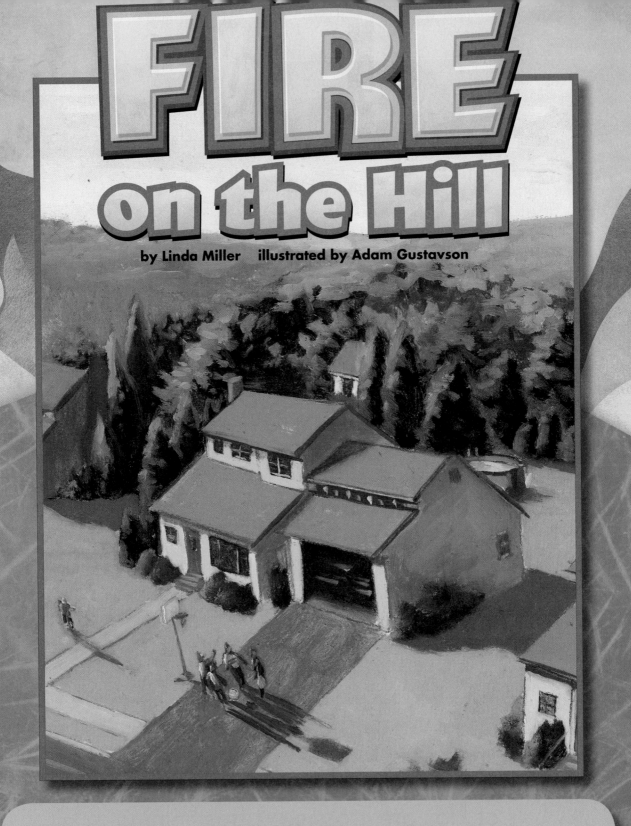

Chuck lives with his mom and dad next to this hill. Chuck has lots of pals on this hill. It is such a grand spot.

Look! Chuck spots fire. Lots are working to stop it. Lots are helping, but they can not act fast enough. It is hot, and nothing can stop it.

Chuck is thinking, "I wish I could help them."
But men in trucks are yelling at him, "You must
run! There is much danger! You must get away fast!"

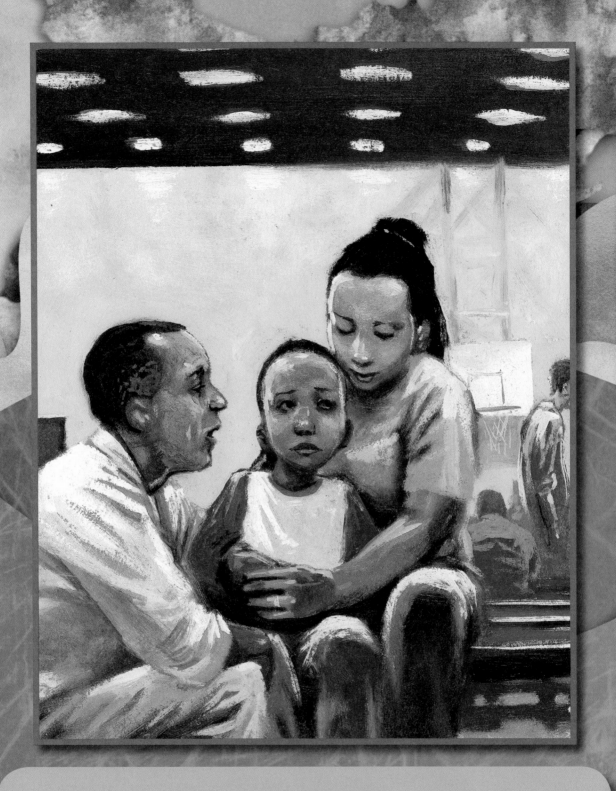

Chuck and his mom and dad run to his school.
Chuck is sad. His mom and dad hug him.
Chuck is resting and thinking.

Chuck spots a bunch of his pals.
Around eight they get good news. The danger is ending. They can go back.

Chuck and his dad are thanking the men for helping them.

Chuck spots a big black patch on his hill. But the fire is not there. The hill will be green soon.

Chuck is glad. Chuck is thinking that his hill is such a grand spot.

Fire Safety
at Home

Make sure you have smoke alarms in your home.

Make a fire escape plan with your family. Practice your escape plan at least twice a year.

In case of a fire, get out of your home. Once you are out, stay out!

Call 9-1-1 from a neighbor's home.

Read Together

24

My New Words

around* The new kids walk **around** school. The top spins **around.**

danger **Danger** is when someone or something can be hurt.

drill When you **drill,** you make a hole in something.

eight* The number between seven and nine is **eight**.

enough* We have **enough** snacks for all.

nothing* There is **nothing** in the empty closet.

patch A **patch** is a piece of ground. A **patch** is also something used to fix a hole or a tear.

*tested high-frequency words

Contents

WORKING TOGETHER LONG AGO

See page 47 for My New Words!

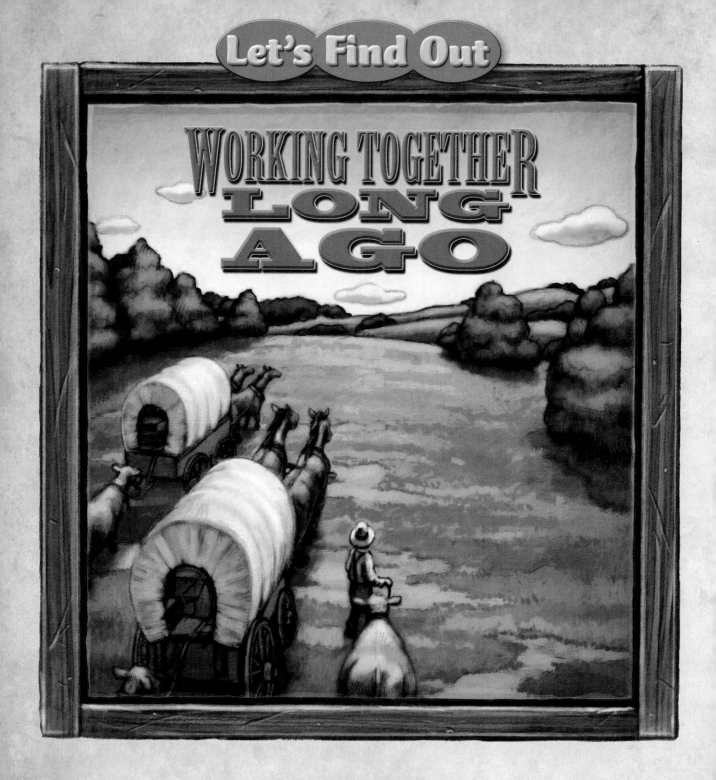

WORKING TOGETHER LONG AGO

CLIP . . . CLOP . . . clip . . . clop! What is that? That is people looking for land. In the past, people went west to get land. This trip was long and filled with risks. It ended at the best spot to build.

Together, people helped change things in this spot. Moms and dads cut and lifted heavy logs and stacked them to build homes. Kids fished and helped carry big pots filled with water.

Soon, this spot had lots of homes. With teams of people, buildings went up fast. This spot got big, big, big!

CLICK . . . CLACK . . . click . . . clack! What is that? That is a train! Trains will bring things to this spot. Trains will bring moms, dads, and kids. This will bring change as well.

The Trip West

by Sue Jacobson

In the past, the trip west was a long, long trip. It lasted many days. People had to stop a lot. What stopped them? Big, big hills and swift water did.

Then some men had this grand plan. Trains run fast on land. Trains can run up hills and over water. Trains can carry heavy things and lots and lots of people. Trains can run west!

But trains must run on tracks. Did the men think of this? Yes! They planned to build lots of tracks. Two teams would do the blasting and chopping and drilling.

Chop! Chop! Chop! Bam! Bam! Bam!
Teams chopped logs and blasted rock. They set tracks up hills and over swift water. Such a big, big job!

Then just a bit of track was left to set.
People clapped and grinned as tracks met at
that last spot.

Now trains packed with people and things were crossing the land. Trains were running up hills and over water. At last, that long, long trip west was fast!

BENJAMIN BANNEKER AND HIS DAD

by Janice Cole
illustrated by Neil Shigley

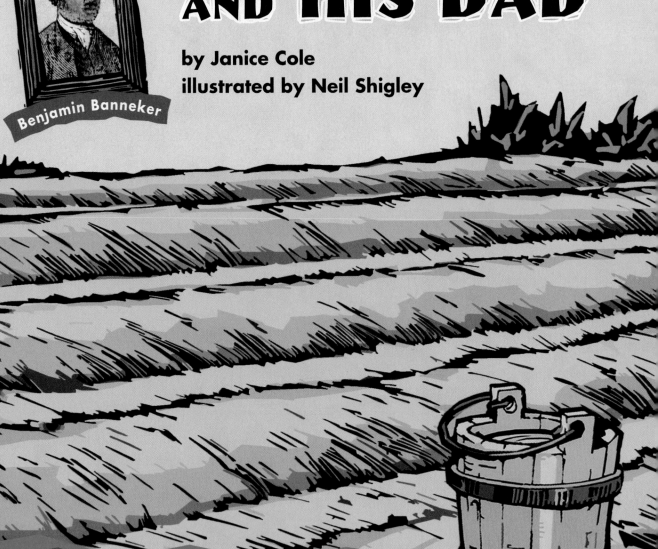

Benjamin Banneker

Dad and Ben worked as a team. When Dad
was digging, Ben helped him. Dig, dig, dig!
As they dug, Ben asked Dad lots of things.
"Dad, what helps plants get big?"

"Well, crops must have sun," Dad said.
Ben looked up and felt hot, hot sun on his
skin. He grinned. "I think the crops will get
lots of sun."

"And crops must get water," Dad said.
"Can you carry that water?"
    Ben yelled, "Yes, yes, I think I can!"
Ben grabbed the water, but could not lift it.
Splish, splash! It spilled.

"This water is heavy," Ben said.
"Yes, but I can fix that," said Dad.
"You can?" Ben asked. "How will you fix it?"

Dad just grinned. "I am thinking of a plan. Help me dig and you will see!"

Dad and Ben dug a long ditch that went to water. The water ran in the ditch.

Then Dad set a plank in that ditch. Dad said, "Planks block the water, Ben. When we lift a plank, then water runs in fast."

Dad lifted a plank and water did run in! The ditch was a big path for running water.

Ben yelled, "Dad, plants can get water now! Plants can get it fast!"

Then Dad and Ben helped others build
ditches, digging and adding planks.

Ben grinned. "We will not get water
for plants as we did in the past. Now we can
just lift a plank!"

Working Together Then and Now

Long ago, families worked together to cook meals.

Today, families work together to cook meals.

Long ago, families worked together to fix things.

Today, families work together to fix things.

46

My New Words

build* To **build** is to make something by putting things together.

carry* When you **carry** something, you take it from one place to another.

heavy* If something is **heavy**, it weighs a lot. It is hard to lift or carry.

home Your **home** is the place where you and your family live.

team A **team** is a group of people working or playing together.

train A **train** is a line of railroad cars pulled by an engine along a track.

water* **Water** is a liquid that fills oceans, rivers, lakes, and ponds. **Water** falls from the sky as rain.

*tested high-frequency words

Contents

Meeting Needs

See page 71 for My New Words!

Meeting Needs

This lot is a mess. It is not a fun spot at all. Can kids help make it a fun spot? Kids can help best if they work together.

This lot needs a new look. It is a big, big job, but kids can lend a hand. What jobs can kids share?

Kids can pick up trash. Yes, they can! One kid can fill a bag. Ten kids can fill ten bags. Pitch in and pick it up! Fill up a few trash bins!

Kids can make this gate look new. Yes, they can! A red gate is fun. Will this bench match? Yes, it will look new as well.

Kids can plant things. Yes, they can! Two kids rake and rake. Another kid digs and digs. Now this lot has a garden!

How will this lot get shade? Kids can plant trees. Yes, they can! This baby tree will grow up, up, up toward the sun.

Kids can set up games. Yes, they can! Grab a pal for a game of catch. Get a bunch of kids together for tag. Take your pick! Games are lots of fun.

Is this the same lot? It does not look the same. It is not a mess. Now it is a fun spot. Kids can enjoy this lot. Yes, they can!

57

The Milk Trade

by Owen James

Dad and Page need milk. This shop sells lots of it. It takes many people to bring milk to this place. Who helps? You will see.

Dave helps. His job is to get the milk. He
wakes up early. He takes the animals to get
milked. Dave enjoys his job. Getting milk is fun.

Grace helps. It is her job to check the milk.
Grace makes sure that milk is safe to drink.
Is this milk safe, Grace?

"Yes," grins Grace. "This milk is safe."

Jake helps. Jake has a big, big truck. He
takes milk from place to place. No need to race,
Jake! This milk is still fresh. The space in back
is chilled.

Min helps. Min has a job in the shop. She sells milk to Dad and Page. Min takes a few bills. Dad gets ten cents back. Thanks, Min!

Dad and Page share this milk.

"Yum!" grins Page. She looks toward Dad. "I will drink another glass!"

Dave, Grace, Jake, and Min help bring milk to Page. Dad helps as well!

THE SNACK STAND

by Mikhail Mokeyev
illustrated by Richard Torrey

SMACK! A kid makes a hit. Another kid makes a run.

"This game is fun," Gage tells Kate. "But we need snacks. And this place has no snacks."

Kate makes her thinking face. "Got it!"
she grins. "We can set up a snack stand!
Lots of kids will enjoy snacks, not just us."

Gage and Kate make a plan. Mom helps them shop. Then they all get to work. Soon, Gage and Kate have lots of snacks to sell.

"We need a place to sell snacks," Kate tells Gage. "In the shade of that tree is best."

"Yes," grins Gage. "That is the best place."

"Fresh snacks for sale!" yells Kate.
A man races toward them. "I will take
that snack and that snack and that snack,"
he tells Gage. The man hands Gage a
few bills. Gage hands the man his snacks.

"Our snack stand is a big hit!" grins Gage.
"Yes," Kate tells him. "But our snack stand
is not the only hit!"
SMACK! Another run!

Lemonade for Sale!

A hot day is a good day to sell lemonade. People will be extra thirsty. Here is how to do it.

1 Decide whether you will make fresh lemonade, frozen lemonade, or lemonade from a mix. What ingredients will you need?

2 Gather supplies. Find a pitcher and cups, a table and chair, and a jar for money.

3 Make an ad for your lemonade. Make a sign that really pops.

4 Set up your stand. It's time to sell!

My New Words

another*   I chose **another** snack.

enjoy*   If you **enjoy** something,
it makes you happy.

few*   If there are a **few**, there are
not many.

need   If you **need** something,
you cannot do without it.

risk   If there is a **risk**, there is a
chance of danger.

share   When you **share**, you let
someone use something.

toward*   He walked **toward** the door.

tree   A **tree** is a large plant with a
trunk, branches, and leaves.

*tested high-frequency words

Contents

Side by Side

See page 99 for My New Words!

73

Side by Side

ants

One ant can not dig this nest. It takes lots and lots of ants instead. This bunch of ants can dig. They make big piles of sand. This will make an ant hill. Ants like to work together.

spittlebug

This bug makes an odd nest on thin twigs.
It has no help. Look at the nest. It is wet. This
bug will hide in its nest. This time one bug can
do just fine.

Kids smile while they rake and fill sacks.
Kids like to make big piles. One kid likes to run
across the grass and dive in big piles.

This place will look fine when they are through. Kids like to work together.

The sun has set. The moon shines. Niles sits at his desk and works on his math.

Niles takes his time. Can Niles add nine plus five? Yes!

Niles will not ask for help. This time one kid can do just fine.

Animals Together, Animals Alone

by Jorge Campa

wolves

Who likes to work together? Who does not? This is a pack. This pack looks out for its pups. The pups like chasing other pups for fun.

This pack likes hunting together. When the pack hunts, it has a plan.

Packs like to sing when the moon is shining.

cougar

Look through the grass. This big cat is hiding.
But it is not resting. Instead, it is hunting. This
big cat does not like hunting with other cats.

It is time to run. This big cat will chase and catch an elk. Run fast, big cat!

penguins

This bunch likes sliding across ice. This bunch likes splashing. This bunch likes diving together and catching fish.

This bunch likes riding on waves for lots and lots of fun. Slide! Splash! Ride!

sloth

This is a sloth. A sloth is not fast. It does not rush. It just hangs from a branch and hides in vines. A sloth is good at taking naps. It is not good at waking up.

A sloth does not spend its time with other sloths. It snacks on buds and twigs. A sloth has an odd life.

SLIDING BOXES

by Elsie Victor

illustrated by R.W. Alley

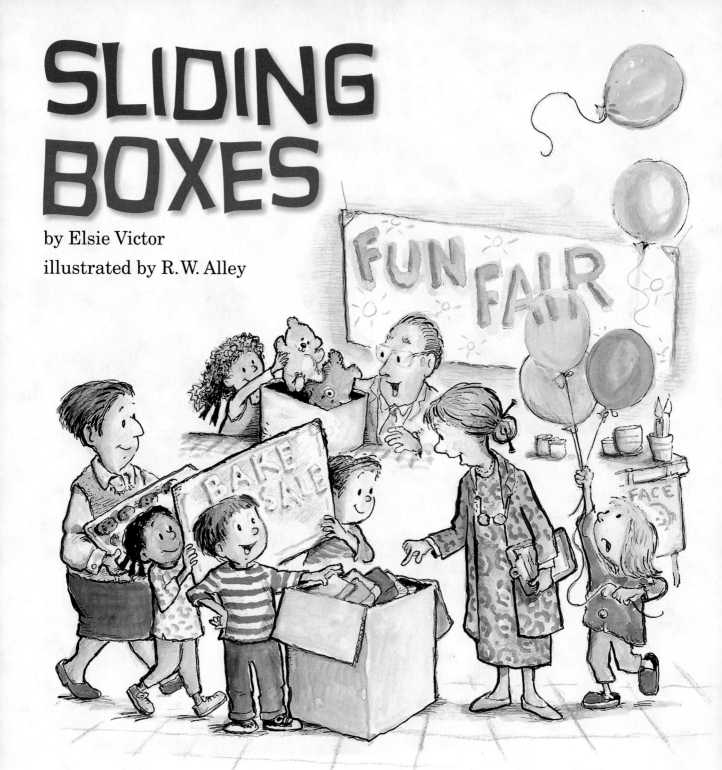

"This big box has things for sale. Mike, can you lift it?" asked Miss Pine. "Can you take it across to the other side?"

"Yes, I can lift it, and I will take it," grinned Mike. "I like to help."

Miss Pine smiled and rushed off.

Mike lifted and lifted. Mike tugged and tugged. The box slid just an inch on the white tile! Mike was tired.

"This will take some time!" said Mike.

Kate waved to Mike. She wanted to help set
up. She grabbed a box with prizes in it.

Kate lifted and lifted. Kate tugged and tugged. Kate was tired.

"This could take till the moon rises! Can I just make this box slide?" Kate asked Mike.

Mike faced Kate.

"I tugged and tugged. This box is not sliding," said Mike. "I will help you with this prize box instead. I have a plan."

Mike placed a line around the box.
"Kate, take this line. Grab an end. We must
slide this box," smiled Mike.

Mike tugged the line. Kate tugged the line.
The box was sliding fast. This plan was wise.
    "When we are through sliding this box, we
can slide mine," smiled Mike.

"We did it! We make a fine team!"
Mike said.

"Yes, but now it is time for fun and games!"
said Kate.

All Work Together

by Woody Guthrie

illustrated by Lynne Avril-Cravath

My mommy told me an' the teacher told me, too,
There's all kinds of work that I can do:
Dry my dishes, sweep my floor,
But if we all work together it won't take very long.

We all work together with a wiggle and a giggle,
We all work together with a giggle and a grin.
We all work together with a wiggle and a giggle,
We all work together with a giggle and a grin.

My daddy said,
And my grandpaw, too,
There's work, worka, work
For me to do.
I can paint my fence.
Mow my lawn.
But if we all work together,
Well, it shouldn't take long. So...

We all work together with a wiggle and a giggle,
We all work together with a giggle and a grin.
We all work together with a wiggle and a giggle,
We all work together with a giggle and a grin.
With a wiggle and a giggle and a google and a goggle
And a jigger and a jagger and a giggle and a grin.

My New Words

across* My friend lives **across** the street.

instead* **Instead** means in place of something else.

moon* The **moon** moves around the Earth.

slide To **slide** is to move in a smooth way. Let's **slide** down the hill.

through* The kitten ran **through** the house. We learned a new song all the way **through**.

tug When you **tug**, you pull hard on something.

*tested high-frequency words

Contents

Working It Out

See page 126 for My New Words!

Working It Out

Cole has a black hat. It is lost in this mess. Jan has tan mittens. But just one. The kids want those things. What can Cole and Jan do?

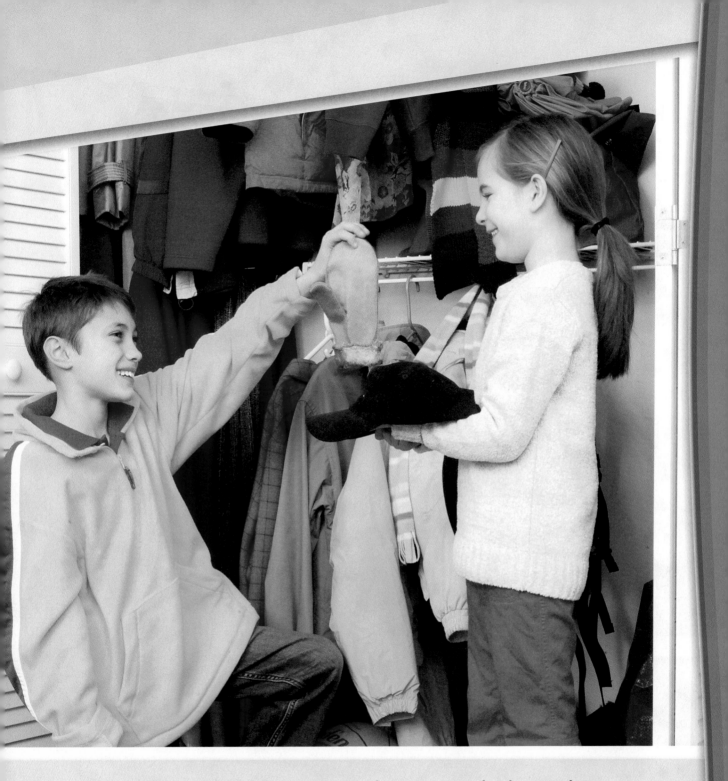

Cole can help Jan and Jan can help Cole.
Together they can get rid of this mess.
Look! A black hat.
Look! A tan mitten.

This class has a pet. Nick jumps up. "I get to give Frog his lunch!"

Then Matt jumps up. "Nope, I get to!"

Frog must eat. What can Nick and Matt do?

6. The adult frog lives on land. It breathes through its lungs and eats insects. Its tail has completely disappeared.

Frog

Nick can help Matt and Matt can help Nick.
Nick gets the bugs. Matt gets the water.
Gulp! At last, Frog is fed!

One slice is left on this plate. Jing snaps, "That slice is mine!"

Lin snaps back, "Do not touch it!"

What can Jing and Lin do?

Jing can help Lin and Lin can help Jing.
A father or mother can help as well!
"Dad, can you cut this slice?" Lin asks.
"That will make two," Jing adds. "Yum!"

"Rose, look at this date!" Kate yells.

"Yikes!" Rose gulps. "We did not remember to get Mother a gift!"

What can Kate and Rose do?

Kate can help Rose and Rose can help Kate. Kate draws Mom sitting on a throne. Rose prints a note. Together they hand Mom their gift. She hugs them close. "You did remember!"

A Note for Stone

by Gabriel Downing ▬ illustrated by Suzanne Beaky

Stone is not at his desk.
"Is Stone not in class?" his pals ask.
"Stone is at home with his father," Miss Jones tells them. "Stone broke his leg."

"Remember when I broke my leg?" Tom asks. "That was not fun!"

Stone's class is sad. They hope Stone will get well fast. "What can we do to help?" asks Pam.

"A get well note is nice," grins Jake.

"Yes!" adds Jen. "I like cats. We can draw cats on Stone's note."

"Stone does not like cats!" Tom snaps. "He will not touch one!"

"Does Stone like dogs?" asks Pam. "He *must* like dogs. I can draw dogs on Stone's note."

"I can not draw dogs," Jake tells Pam. "But I can draw balloons."

What can this class do?

Nate has a plan. "We can make lots of notes for Stone!"
The kids smile. They like this plan.

The class makes lots of notes. Jen's note has a cat. Pam's note has a dog. Jake's note has a whole lot of balloons.

Stone's mother takes the notes to him. Stone sends just one note back.

The Balloon Ride

by Victor Strong
illustrated by Jeff Ebbeler

Rose will be nine. Rose and her pals will have fun at Rose's home. Meg has a gift for Rose.
"I hope Rose has cake and games," said Meg.

"I will get red and pink and white," said Meg. "I remember that Rose likes those. I will get this balloon too. And this. And this. And this. Then I must rush to Rose's home. I can not miss the fun."

This man has balloons too. Meg chose
five. Then she chose another. And another.
And another. Now Meg did not have just six
balloons. She did not have just nine. She had
lots and lots and lots!

Meg held those balloons' strings. Then she
felt them tug and lift. Meg rose up, up, up.

Meg rode past the gates and past the lake.
"I will not get to Rose's home like this," said
Meg. "I will pass it. I will not get this gift to
Rose. I will miss games and cake."

Just then Meg spotted gulls. She looked at the gulls' bills. Those gulls could poke holes in Meg's balloons. That would help a lot.

"Help!" Meg yelled. "Can you help?"

The gulls went past Meg. Peck, peck, pop! Peck, pop, pop!

At last Meg touched the grass. She landed at
Rose's home.

"I made it!" said Meg. "I hope I am not late.
I hope I did not miss games and cake."

"You are not late. But is this a new way to ride?" joked Rose's mother and father.

"It is fun with help from gulls!" Meg grinned. "But next time I will get just five balloons!"

Make a Greeting Card

You will need:

colored paper

crayons or markers

1 Fold a sheet of paper in half.

2 Write a greeting, such as Happy Birthday, on the front.

3 Draw a picture on the front.

4 Write a note inside the card. You can draw a picture here too. Sign your name.

5 Give the card to your friend!

My New Words

balloon

A **balloon** is a toy made of thin rubber and filled with air or gas.

father*

A **father** is a man who has a child or children.

gull

A **gull** is a bird that lives near lakes and oceans.

mother*   A **mother** is a woman who has a child or children.

remember*   When you **remember** something, you keep it in your mind.

throne   A **throne** is a chair on which a king or a queen sits.

touch*   When you **touch** something, you feel it.

*tested high-frequency words

Acknowledgments

Text

Every effort has been made to locate the copyright owner of material reproduced in this component. Omissions brought to our attention will be corrected in subsequent editions. Grateful acknowledgment is made to the following for copyrighted material.

96 Ludlow Music, Inc. c/o TRO (The Richmond Organization) "All Work Together" words and music by Woody Guthrie. TRO Copyright © 1956 (Renewed) and 1963 (Renewed) Folkways Music Publishers, Inc., New York, NY. Used by Permission.

Illustrations

Cover: Lynne Avril-Cravath, Robert W. Alley; **2, 5–11** Kim Behm; **2, 96–98** Lynne Avril-Cravath; **3, 116–126** Jeff Ebbeler; **3, 72–73, 88–95** R. W. Alley; **5, 16–23** Adam Gustavson; **26–27, 38–45** Neil Shigley; **28–31** Guy Porfirio; **49, 64–69** Richard Torrey; **70** Holli Conger; **97** Philomena O'Neill; **101, 110–115** Suzanne Beaky.

Photographs

Every effort has been made to secure permission and provide appropriate credit for photographic material. The publisher deeply regrets any omission and pledges to correct errors called to its attention in subsequent editions.

Unless otherwise acknowledged, all photographs are the property of Pearson Education, Inc.

Photo locators denoted as follows: Top (T), Center (C), Bottom (B), Left (L), Right (R), Background (Bkgd)

Cover: (CR) ©Jeff Vanuga/Corbis, (CR) ©ThinkStock/SuperStock, (BL) Stockbyte/Getty Images; **1** Getty Images; **4** (C) ©Spencer Grant/PhotoEdit; **12** (T) ©Michael Pole/Corbis; **13** (T) ©Robert Brenner/PhotoEdit; **14** (T) ©PIXFOLIO/Alamy; **15** (T) ©Spencer Grant/PhotoEdit; **27** (CR) ©The Granger Collection, NY; **32** (BL) ©Oscar Williams/Alamy Images, (C) ©The Granger Collection, NY; **33** (BR) ©Oscar Williams/Alamy Images, (BR) ©Russ Bishop/Alamy Images; **34** (C) ©The Granger Collection, NY, (BL) Getty Images; **35** (B) ©David Brimm/Alamy; **36** (C) The Granger Collection, New York; **37** (BR) ©The Granger Collection, NY; **38** (T) ©The Granger Collection, NY; **46** (BR) ©Bill Bachmann/Alamy Images, (CR) ©Ryan McVay/Getty Images, (BR, BL) ©The Granger Collection, NY; **48** (C) ©Jim West/Alamy Images; **49** (CR) ©Robert Polett/AGStockUSA; **50** (C) Getty Images; **51** (TR) ©Ian Logan/Getty Images; **52** (C) ©Corbis/SuperStock, (CL) ©Jim West/Alamy Images; **53** (C) ©Angela Wyant/Getty Images, (TR) ©David McNew /Getty Images; **54** (C) ©Bloomimage/Getty Images, (C) ©Don Smetzer/PhotoEdit, Inc., (CL) ©Jeff Greenberg/PhotoEdit, Inc., (C) ©Jim West/Alamy Images; **55** (TR) Epcot Images/Alamy; **56** (B) ©iofoto/Fotolia, (C) ©Tony Freeman/PhotoEdit, Inc.; **57** (B) ©Don Farrall/Getty Images; **59** (T) ©Robert Polett/AGStockUSA; **60** (T) ©Arman Weigel/dpa/Corbis; **61** (T) ©John Gress/Reuters/Corbis; **62** (T) ©Emmerich and Webb/Image Source; **71** (B) ©Nic Miller/Organics Image Library/Alamy; **73** (TR) ©Bruce Coleman, Inc. /Alamy Images; **74** (C) ©James L. Amos/Corbis; **75** (C) ©Bruce Coleman, Inc. /Alamy Images; **76** (TL) ©IT Stock Free/SuperStock, (CR) ©Steve Skjold / Alamy Images; **77** (C) ©ThinkStock/SuperStock; **80** (T) ©Tom Brakefield/Corbis; **81** (T) ©Jeff Vanuga/Corbis; **82** (C) ©Digistock/Alamy; **83** (C) ©Tom Brakefield/Corbis; **84** (T) ©Steve Bloom Images / Alamy Images; **85** (T) ©Danita Delimont /Alamy Images; **86** (T) ©Buddy Mays/Corbis; **87** (C) ©Bryan Lowry /Alamy Images; **127** (BR) ©Toledano/Getty Images.